IIX 5/15 LT 5/14

WITHDRAWN

ID0576686

HISTORIC CIVILIZATIONS

Medieval Europe

Susie Hodge

GARETH**STEVENS**
GS
PUBLISHING
A World Almanac Education Group Company

How to use this book

Each topic in this book is clearly labeled and contains all these components:

Topic heading

Introduction to the topic

Subtopic 1 gives information about one aspect of the topic.

Words that are in the topic glossary are bolded the first time they appear on the page.

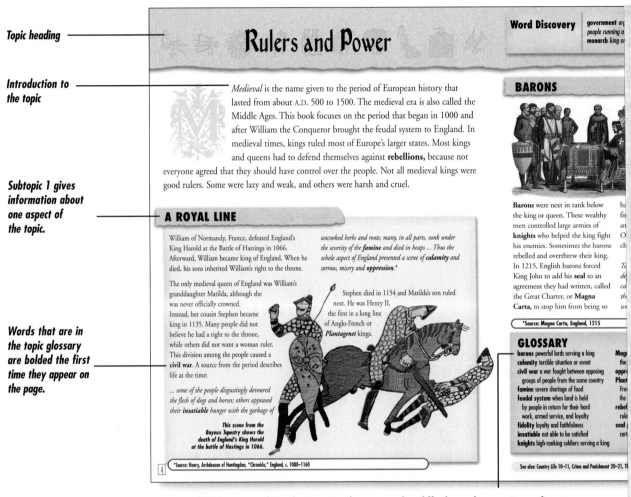

Rulers and Power

Medieval is the name given to the period of European history that lasted from about A.D. 500 to 1500. The medieval era is also called the Middle Ages. This book focuses on the period that began in 1000 and after William the Conqueror brought the feudal system to England. In medieval times, kings ruled most of Europe's larger states. Most kings and queens had to defend themselves against **rebellions,** because not everyone agreed that they should have control over the people. Not all medieval kings were good rulers. Some were lazy and weak, and others were harsh and cruel.

A ROYAL LINE

William of Normandy, France, defeated England's King Harold at the Battle of Hastings in 1066. Afterward, William became king of England. When he died, his sons inherited William's right to the throne.

The only medieval queen of England was William's granddaughter Matilda, although she was never officially crowned. Instead, her cousin Stephen became king in 1135. Many people did not believe he had a right to the throne, while others did not want a woman ruler. This division among the people caused a **civil war.** A source from the period describes life at the time:

*... some of the people disgustingly devoured the flesh of dogs and horses; others appeased their **insatiable** hunger with the garbage of*

*uncooked herbs and roots; many, in all parts, sunk under the severity of the **famine** and died in heaps ... Thus the whole aspect of England presented a scene of **calamity** and sorrow, misery and **oppression**.**

Stephen died in 1154 and Matilda's son ruled next. He was Henry II, the first in a long line of Anglo-French or ***Plantagenet*** kings.

This scene from the Bayeux Tapestry shows the death of England's King Harold at the battle of Hastings in 1066.

Source: Henry, Archdeacon of Huntingdon, "Chronicle," England, c. 1080–1160

4

Word Discovery

government or...
people running a...
monarch king or...

BARONS

Barons were next in rank below the king or queen. These wealthy men controlled large armies of **knights** who helped the king fight his enemies. Sometimes the barons rebelled and overthrew their king. In 1215, English barons forced King John to add his **seal** to an agreement they had written, called the Great Charter, or **Magna Carta**, to stop him from being so

Source: Magna Carta, England, 1215

GLOSSARY

barons powerful lords serving a king
calamity terrible situation or event
civil war a war fought between opposing groups of people from the same country
famine severe shortage of food
feudal system when land is held by people in return for their hard work, armed service, and loyalty
fidelity loyalty and faithfulness
insatiable not able to be satisfied
knights high-ranking soldiers serving a king

See also: Country Life 10–11, Crime and Punishment 20–21, Th...

The Glossary explains the meaning of any unusual or difficult words appearing on these two pages.

Please visit our web site at: www.garethstevens.com
For a free color catalog describing Gareth Stevens Publishing's list of high-quality books and multimedia programs, call 1-800-542-2595 (USA) or 1-800-387-3178 (Canada). Gareth Stevens Publishing's fax: (414) 332-3567.

Library of Congress Cataloging-in-Publication Data

Hodge, Susie, 1960-
    Medieval Europe / by Susie Hodge.
        p. cm. — (Historic civilizations)
    Includes index.
    ISBN 0-8368-4202-2 (lib. bdg.)
    1. Civilization, Medieval—Juvenile literature. I. Title. II. Series.
CB351.H55 2004
940.1—dc22   2004045301

This North American edition first published in 2005 by
Gareth Stevens Publishing
A World Almanac Education Group Company
330 West Olive Street, Suite 100
Milwaukee, Wisconsin 53212 USA

This U.S. edition copyright © 2005 by Gareth Stevens, Inc. Original edition copyright © 2004 ticktock Entertainment Ltd. First published in Great Britain in 2004 as *Your Medieval Homework Helper* by ticktock Media Ltd., Unit 2, Orchard Business Centre, North Farm Road, Tunbridge Wells, Kent TN23XF, UK.

The publishers wish to thank Meme Ltd., Andrew Reynolds, Richard Tames, and Egan-Reid Ltd. for their research and consulting expertise in the making of this book.

Gareth Stevens editor: Barbara Kiely Miller
Gareth Stevens cover design: Steve Schraenkler

Printed in the United States of America

1 2 3 4 5 6 7 8 9 08 07 06 05 04

Contents

Rulers and Power   4

Religion   6

Town Life   8

Country Life   10

Death   12

Food and Drink   14

Health and Medicine   16

Men and Women   18

Crime and Punishments   20

The Crusades   22

Art   24

Buildings   26

Trade, Craft, and Communications   28

Penance and Pilgrimages   30

Index & Time Line   32

Subtopic 2 gives information about another aspect of the topic.

Discover other words that relate to the topic.

The Case Study is a closer look at a famous person, artifact, or building that relates to the topic.

Each photo or illustration is described and discussed in the accompanying text.

Captions clearly explain what is in the picture.

At the bottom of some sections, a reference bar tells where the information has come from.

Other pages in the book that relate to what you have read in this topic are listed here.

A reference bar marked with an asterisk (*) gives the source of the quotations in the text.

---

person who rules an empire or kingdom

nobility class of people of high rank or wealth

overthrow remove from power

peasants poor farmers

The barons made King John seal the Magna Carta in 1215 as a promise to be just to his people.

y. This was the to specify the rights English people. s included in the

m we have ssessed of lands, or rights, without ent of his equals, estore these.*

t that set out England njust use of power n to the Anglo- d queens during

g against their

mped into wax to ters or documents

dings 26–27

CASE STUDY

The Feudal System

King William I introduced the **feudal system** to England. This system organized power and land and divided people into classes: The king, who originally owned all the land, gave some land to the church and to the barons. In return for large blocks of land, the barons promised to fight for the king. They then lent some of their land to knights who also promised to fight for the king. These knights then lent some of their land to the common people and promised to take care of them if the people took care of the land. People had to take an oath of **fidelity** with which they promised to abide by the rules of the feudal system. Here is part of one such oath:

I promise on my faith that I will in future be faithful to count William, and will observe my homage to him completely against all persons in good faith and without deceit.*

This illustration from 1469 shows Jean de Sainte-Maure making the oath of fidelity to become a baron.

*Source: Galbert de Bruges, "Homage and Fealty to the Count of Flanders" from "Chronicle of the Death of Charles the Good," Belgium, 1127

Rulers and Power

Medieval is the name given to the period of European history that lasted from about A.D. 500 to 1500. The medieval era is also called the Middle Ages. This book focuses on the period that began in 1000 and after William the Conqueror brought the feudal system to England. In medieval times, kings ruled most of Europe's larger states. Most kings and queens had to defend themselves against **rebellions,** because not everyone agreed that they should have control over the people. Not all medieval kings were good rulers. Some were lazy and weak, and others were harsh and cruel.

A ROYAL LINE

William of Normandy, France, defeated England's King Harold at the Battle of Hastings in 1066. Afterward, William became king of England. When he died, his sons inherited William's right to the throne.

The only medieval queen of England was William's granddaughter Matilda, although she was never officially crowned. Instead, her cousin Stephen became king in 1135. Many people did not believe he had a right to the throne, while others did not want a woman ruler. This division among the people caused a **civil war**. A source from the period describes life at the time:

*... some of the people disgustingly devoured the flesh of dogs and horses; others appeased their **insatiable** hunger with the garbage of uncooked herbs and roots; many, in all parts, sunk under the severity of the **famine** and died in heaps ... Thus the whole aspect of England presented a scene of **calamity** and sorrow, misery and **oppression**.** *

Stephen died in 1154 and Matilda's son ruled next. He was Henry II, the first in a long line of Anglo-French or *Plantagenet* kings.

This scene from the Bayeux Tapestry shows the death of England's King Harold at the battle of Hastings in 1066.

*Source: Henry, Archdeacon of Huntingdon, "Chronicle," England, c. 1080–1160

Word Discovery

government *organization and people running a country*
monarch *king or queen;*

person who rules an empire or kingdom
nobility *class of people of high*

rank or wealth
overthrow *remove from power*
peasants *poor farmers*

BARONS

The barons made King John seal the Magna Carta in 1215 as a promise to be just to his people.

Barons were next in rank below the king or queen. These wealthy men controlled large armies of **knights** who helped the king fight his enemies. Sometimes the barons rebelled and overthrew their king. In 1215, English barons forced King John to add his **seal** to an agreement they had written, called the Great Charter, or **Magna Carta,** to stop him from being so harsh and greedy. This was the first document to specify the rights and freedoms of English people. One of the rights included in the charter stated:

*To any man whom we have deprived or dispossessed of lands, castles, liberties, or rights, without the lawful judgement of his equals, we will at once restore these.**

*Source: Magna Carta, England, 1215

GLOSSARY

barons powerful lords serving a king
calamity terrible situation or event
civil war a war fought between opposing groups of people from the same country
famine severe shortage of food
feudal system when land is held by people in return for their hard work, armed service, and loyalty
fidelity loyalty and faithfulness
insatiable not able to be satisfied
knights high-ranking soldiers serving a king

Magna Carta document that set out the rights of people in England
oppression harsh and unjust use of power
Plantagenet name given to the Anglo-French line of kings and queens during the Middle Ages
rebellions people fighting against their rulers
seal person's symbol stamped into wax to certify or authorize letters or documents

See also: Country Life 10–11, Crime and Punishment 20–21, The Crusades 22–23, Buildings 26–27

CASE STUDY

The Feudal System

King William I introduced the **feudal system** to England. This system organized power and land and divided people into classes: The king, who originally owned all the land, gave some land to the church and to the barons. In return for large blocks of land, the barons promised to fight for the king. They then lent some of their land to knights who also promised to fight for the king. These knights then lent some of their land to the common people and promised to take care of them if the people took care of the land. People had to take an oath of **fidelity** with which they promised to abide by the rules of the feudal system. Here is part of one such oath:

*I promise on my faith that I will in future be faithful to count William, and will observe my homage to him completely against all persons in good faith and without deceit.**

This illustration from 1469 shows Jean de Sainte-Maure making the oath of fidelity to become a baron.

*Source: Galbert de Bruges, "Homage and Fealty to the Count of Flanders" from "Chronicle of the Death of Charles the Good," Belgium, 1127

Religion

People believed that God controlled everything. The dominant religion in much of Europe was Christianity, which was divided between **Orthodox** Christianity in eastern Europe and Catholicism in western Europe. Christian churches had great power and influence during the Middle Ages. Church leaders, such as bishops and archbishops, played leading roles in the government. The archbishop was the chief bishop and ruled over the bishops in a wide area. Bishops, who were often wealthy and came from noble families, ruled over groups of parishes called **dioceses**.

PEOPLE IN THE CHURCH

Priests led the church service, called the *Mass*, in towns and villages throughout Europe. People visited priests to confess their sins, and the priest could forgive them on God's behalf.

Like priests, some men and women chose to devote their lives to God. They became monks and nuns and lived in religious communities called monasteries and convents. Also like priests, neither monks nor nuns were allowed to marry. They took vows to own nothing and to do whatever the **abbot** or **abbess** told them. They spent Sundays praying and divided their time on other days between prayer, study, and work. Their work might include copying manuscripts and decorating them with **illuminated** letters, cooking, cleaning, or working in the fields. Some monks and nuns ran schools or cared for the sick, and others simply spent their lives praying. St. Francis was a monk who founded an order of friars called the Franciscans.

Although many people at the time could not read or write, most religious figures could, as represented by this thirteenth century Italian painting of St. Peter the Martyr, who was killed in 1252.

Unlike many other religious orders, the Franciscans did not have to live confined to monasteries. St. Francis wrote this advice to fellow friars:

*I worked with my hands, and want to do so still. And I definitely want all the other brothers to work at some honest job. Those who don't know how should learn, not because they want to receive wages but as an example and to avoid idleness.**

*Source: St Francis, "Testament," Italy, 1226

Word Discovery

devout *deeply religious*
eternal *never ending, forever*
Latin *the language of ancient*

Romans that is spoken in some
Catholic church services
parish priest *priest of one*

or more churches in an area
penance *punishment for sins*
repent *being sorry for misdeeds*

HEAVEN AND HELL

People believed that when they died, they went to **purgatory**, where God decided whether they should be sent to heaven or hell. In order to move from purgatory to heaven, a person had to have lived an honest life. Medieval visions of heaven and hell were painted on the walls of churches to remind people to be good. An Italian writer named Dante Alighieri wrote an **epic** poem called *The Divine Comedy* that gave vivid descriptions of hell, such as this one:

These wretches, who ne'er lived, Went on in nakedness, and sorely stung; By wasps and hornets, which bedew'd their cheeks; With blood, that, mix'd with tears, dropp'd to their feet, And by disgustful worms was gather'd there.*

Images of hell, like the one in this fifteenth-century French painting, appeared on the walls of churches to warn people about hell.

*Source: Dante Alighieri, "The Divine Comedy," Italy, 1313

Glossary

abbot (or abbess) head of a monastery (or convent)
baptized admitted into the Christian faith through a ritual ceremony using water
diocese group of parishes, or local church communities, that a bishop is in charge of
epic long poem about a hero; artwork or event of great length
illuminated decorated with beautiful colors,

letters, or pictures and used in manuscripts
Mass Catholic Christian church service
Orthodox traditional form of Christianity in Eastern Europe
purgatory place for suffering and penance before entering heaven or hell after death
wattle and daub twigs woven together, coated with a mixture of mud or clay, horsehair, and straw, and used in building

CASE STUDY

Churches

The church was always located in the center of a town or village because it was the most important part of medieval life. Every day, wherever they were, people heard the church bells ringing every hour. The bells were supposed to remind them of their duty to God. When people were born, they were **baptized** in the church, and they worshiped at Mass throughout their lives. They got married in the church and, at the end of their lives, they were buried in the churchyard. Rich people might be buried under finely carved stone monuments, while the poor were buried in unmarked graves. Churches were usually built from stone, at a time when most other buildings were made of wood or **wattle and daub**.

The church was the biggest building in a medieval town. This one is in the English town of Lyddington.

See also: Health and Medicine 16–17, Art 24–25, Buildings 26–27, Penance and Pilgrimages 30–31

Town Life

In medieval times, there were far fewer towns than there are today and not many big cities. Some medieval cities had drainage systems, although in most towns water had to be carried to each house from wells. Towns were busy places. Farmers herded **livestock** or drove carts through the streets. People went to towns to buy and sell goods at the **markets**. Gradually, more people moved to the towns, often to learn the crafts or trades that were becoming so popular.

MARKETS

In the Middle Ages, everything was made by hand, from shoes to furniture. **Tradespeople** who made handcrafted items included weavers, dyers, candlemakers, carpenters, blacksmiths, tailors, and goldsmiths.

Boys and girls who began learning these skills at a young age were known as **apprentices**. Most peasants went to market every week in their nearest town. They sold food produced at home, such as vegetables or eggs. Some of them set up stalls with prepared food for sale, and others sold goods they had bought from craftspeople or **merchants**. Markets had a reputation, however, for being unholy places, as described in this account:

They are held on feast days, and men miss thereby the divine office and the sermon and even disobey the precept of hearing Mass, and attend these meetings against the Church's commands. Sometimes, too, they are held in graveyards and other holy places. Frequently you will hear men swearing there: "By God I will not give you so much for it," or "By God I will not take a smaller price," or "By God it is not worth so much as that"... sometimes, too, quarrels happen and violent disputes ...*

Traders and craftspeople sold many things at the market, such as food, pots, shoes, and hats.

*Source: Humbert de Romans, "On Markets & Fairs," France, c. 1270

Word Discovery

hygiene *cleanliness and other healthy practices*
illiterate *unable to read or write*

inns *places with sleeping rooms and food for travelers*
journeyman *fully trained*

craftsperson who worked for a master craftsperson
sewers *waste disposal system*

DAILY LIFE

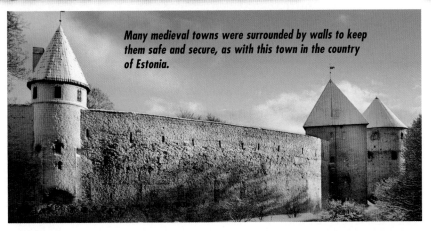

Many medieval towns were surrounded by walls to keep them safe and secure, as with this town in the country of Estonia.

Many medieval towns were surrounded by stone walls. These gave a town security and helped the authorities know who was coming into town so that they could charge visitors a tax. Streets were usually narrow, cramped, and dirty, especially on market days when traders, shoppers, beggars, thieves, farmers, and animals all traveled on them. The layout of medieval markets can be guessed by looking at street names that still exist, such as Baker Street, Tanner Street, Pudding Lane, and Fish Row. In Oxford, for example, Beef Lane is next to the southern gate of the town. Historians believe that this was where live cattle were once brought to town and slaughtered. Many streets had shops on each side that opened at the front to sell goods directly to customers. Most people could not read, so shop signs had to have pictures in them: a boot would hang above a cobbler's shop, and a green bush was the sign of an inn.

Glossary

apprentices young people who learn craft skills from a master-craftsman in his shop or home
fortress a strong structure, sometimes including a town, that is secure against military attack
livestock farm animals

markets places for buying and selling
merchants people who buy or sell goods
traders another name for merchants
tradespeople people who traded with others, shopkeepers
traitors people who carry out crimes against their country or rulers

CASE STUDY

London

The city of London grew along the banks of the river Thames. As with other towns, a high stone wall surrounded the city. Despite living in the largest city in medieval England, a person could walk from one side of London to the other in twenty minutes. The Tower of London was built in the 1070s as a **fortress**, palace, and prison. Between 1176 and 1209, a nineteen-arch stone bridge was built across the Thames. It was named London Bridge, and it included houses, shops, and a chapel. Fairs and markets were held on the bridge, at which the chopped-off heads of **traitors** were put on display.

Many criminals were imprisoned, tortured, and executed in the Tower of London during the medieval period.

See also: Death 12–13, Crime and Punishment 20–21, Buildings 26–27, Trade, Craft, and Communications 28–29

Country Life

Nine out of ten people in medieval England were peasants who lived in the countryside. Most of them worked on the land as part of the feudal system and paid a tax to the church called a *tithe*. **Peasants** usually worked extremely hard. There were many jobs to do all year long on medieval farms, such as caring for animals, **plowing** fields, and **harvesting** crops.

FARMING

Farm fields around medieval villages did not look like most European fields today, because farming at that time was done differently.

This Italian painting of a peasant woman feeding grain to roosters is from the fourteenth century.

Most fields were open and not surrounded by hedges or fences. Peasants grew crops, such as wheat, oats, peas, beans, and barley. Animals were kept on the **manor** and looked after by the villagers, including oxen, cows, sheep, goats, pigs, geese, and hens. Sheep were kept for their wool, and most peasants **sheared** their sheep in the summer. Other animals were raised for their meat, milk, and eggs, as well as their skins, which were tanned and made into clothing and other goods. Many details about medieval farming were learned from surviving texts, such as this one offering advice to farmers:

When your lambs are yeaned let the shepherd take away the wool about the teats, for often it happens that the wool adheres to the mouths of the lambs from the teats, and they swallow it, and it remains in their stomachs, and thereby many have died.*

*Source: Walter of Henley, "Treatise on Husbandry," England, c. 1270

Word Discovery

agriculture *farming*
boundary *something marking a limit, such as a line or a place*

rustic *related to the countryside*
sickles *sharp, hook-shaped tools for cutting grain*

threshing *beating the grain in order to separate the grain from the stalks*

HARD WORK

Peasants worked hard on the land nearly every day of the year.

All farm work was done by hand using simple tools. Most farm jobs involved hard, physical work, such as hoeing crops, shearing sheep, carrying manure, plowing, and harvesting. Peasants labored every day except Sundays and holy days, no matter what the weather was like. Most villages had a blacksmith, a carpenter, and others with special jobs. Most country folk, however, were terribly poor and hungry. Many of them caught wild animals from the lord's estate, but if they were caught, they would be severely punished. An anonymous document from the period describes how much a farm laborer should be paid:

*You can well have three acres weeded for a penny, and an acre of meadow mown for fourpence, and an acre of waste meadow for threepence-**halfpenny**, and an acre of meadow turned and raised for a penny-halfpenny, and an acre of waste for a penny-**farthing**.**

*Source: Walter of Henley, "Treatise on Husbandry," England, c. 1270

Glossary

anonymous unknown name or identity
farthing coin worth quarter of a penny
halfpenny coin worth half a penny
harvesting gathering crops
manor a block of land under the control of one lord and his agent
peasants poor farmers or farm laborers

plowing turning over the land for farming
shearing clipping the wool off sheep
tithe a tax that medieval people had to pay the village priest: one-tenth of their farm produce; today, to tithe is to give a voluntary donation of one-tenth of one's income to a church or other group

CASE STUDY

This twelfth-to-thirteenth-century manor house in Shropshire, England, is where the lord and lady would have lived.

The Manor House

The **manor** was a sizable piece of land with a large house where the lord and lady of the manor lived. In return for the right to live in the manor house, the lord or lady would pledge their loyalty to the baron, who was an even greater landowner. Sometimes, the baron would send someone else to check on how the lord was running the manor. Here is a description of a baron's expectations:

*... if there be any cheating in the sowing, or plowing, or reaping, he shall easily see it. And he must cause all the meadows and several pastures to be measured by acres, and thereby can one know the cost, and how much hay is necessary every year for the sustenance of the manor ...**

The lord expected the villagers to work on his land in order to receive a house and land of their own, too.

*Source: **Anonymous,** "The Seneschaucy," England, c. 1270

See also: Rulers and Power 4–5, Death 12–13, Buildings 26–27, Trade, Craft, and Communications 28–29

Death

People in the Middle Ages had an average **life expectancy** of between thirty and thirty-five years. War, **famine**, and disease claimed thousands of lives. Widespread **poverty** meant that many houses were overcrowded and that people were living on the streets. All of these things contributed to disease and early death. From studying their skeletons, archaeologists have learned that many medieval peasants had worn-out joints and deformities caused by many years of hard work. Their bones also revealed how people died, many of them from infectious diseases like the plague.

SHORT LIVES

The most common causes of death were dirty water and bad **hygiene**, especially in the crowded, dirty towns. Poor diet was another big reason.

People did not drink or eat enough dairy products, and this meant that their **immunity** was low. A newborn baby and/or its mother had a high risk of dying during childbirth because of bad hygiene, too. Very few things — people's bodies, the streets, or houses — were clean, and certainly not by today's standards. Other common diseases included tuberculosis, dysentery, and smallpox. There was not a good system for getting rid of sewage, such as there is today. Human waste flowed in the ditches alongside the roads, and people sometimes went to the toilet out of their windows if they couldn't be bothered going to the **privy**! In 1349, Edward III made a complaint to the Mayor of London about the city's dirty streets being directly related to the spread of disease:

This was a common scene in the fourteenth century: A doctor tends to a dying man as a priest reads the last rites — a church ritual prayed before someone's death.

Cause the human faeces and other filth lying in the streets and lanes in the city to be removed with all speed to places far distant, so that no greater cause of mortality may arise from such smells.*

*Source: Edward III, Letter to Mayor of London, England, 1349

Word Discovery

contagious *(disease) capable of being passed among people*
epidemic *spreading*

quickly through a community, such as a widespread disease
execution *carrying out a*

sentence of death
flout *disregard, insult, or reject something, such as rules*

THE PLAGUE

Between 1347 and 1349, the **bubonic plague,** or Black Death, killed about one in three people across Europe. The plague spread quickly, and no one knew how to cure it. Few people who caught it survived for more than about three days. Many people believed that the plague was a punishment from God. A source from the period describes what happened when a person got the disease:

This French painting from 1499 shows St. Sebastian appearing to victims of the plague.

Many would meet their end in the public streets both day and night, and many others, who met their ends in their own houses, would first come to the attention of their neighbors because of the stench of their rotting corpses more than anything else; and with these and others all dying, there were corpses everywhere. *

*Source: Boccaccio, "The Decameron," Italy, 1348

Glossary

bubonic plague a disease caused by a bacteria affecting huge numbers of people; also called the *Black Death*
chrism a type of holy oil used in church sacraments
consecrated made sacred
famine severe shortage of food; starving
hygiene cleanliness and healthy practices
immunity the body's natural defense

against disease and illness
impious disrespectful of God or parents
life expectancy the normal length of time a person is expected to live
poverty condition of being poor
privy an outdoor room where people went to the toilet
sacrificial lamb Christian term for a person sacrificed for God; also name for Jesus

See also: Religion 6–7, Town Life 8–9, Country Life 10–11, Health and Medicine 16–17

CASE STUDY

Murder!

In 1162, Henry II chose his close friend Thomas Becket to become the Archbishop of Canterbury. Thomas believed his new position meant that his duty to the church must now come before his duty to the king. His change in loyalty made the king angry, causing some of Henry's knights to go to Canterbury, where they murdered Thomas on the steps of the altar in the cathedral. An eyewitness account reported Thomas Becket's death:

*... the **impious** knight, fearing that [Thomas] would be saved by the people and escape alive, suddenly set upon him and, shaving off the summit of his crown which the sacred **chrism consecrated** to God, he wounded the **sacrificial lamb** of God in the head ...* *

This picture from a medieval manuscript shows Thomas Becket turning his back on royal power.

*Source: Edward Grim, "The Murder of Thomas Becket," England, 1170

Food and Drink

People living in medieval Europe ate quite unhealthy diets. For example, they believed that fresh fruit was harmful. Rich people could afford a wide range of food, such as dried fruit, meats, sauces, puddings, nuts, and cream. Peasants ate the food that they grew. **Archaeologists** have discovered what people ate by uncovering the remains of medieval meals at **excavation** sites. The remains were there because people used to get rid of their garbage by simply throwing it into pits behind their houses.

WHAT THEY ATE

The rich ate fresh meats that had been roasted on **spits** over fires, such as **venison**, chicken, and goose. In winter, they ate salted meat, often in a stew. Large towns had inns that sold carry-out food, such as *hot thrush* or *hot sheep's foot*.

Poor people ate a kind of stew called *pottage* made from peas, beans, and onions that they grew. The only sweet foods that the poor ate were the berries, nuts, and honey that they collected from the woods.

Many recipes from the Middle Ages survive. Here is a medieval recipe for Puddyng of Purpaysse (Stuffed Porpoise Stomach):

*Take the Blood of him, & the grease of him self, & Oatmeal, & Salt, & Pepper, & Ginger, & mix these together well, & then put this in the Gut of the porpoise, & then let it boil easily, & not hard, a good while; & then take him up, & broil him a little, & then serve forth.**

Servants are depicted preparing suckling pigs for the lord's table at a manor house.

*Source: Recipe for "Puddyng of Purpaysse," *Harleian MS 279*, England, c. 1430

Word Discovery

banquet *feast*
earthenware *clay pottery*
pitcher *big cooking pot on legs*

scullion *kitchen helper who washes dishes and helps the cook*
skillet *frying pan*

trenchers *thick slices of bread used as plates by the rich that were then eaten by the poor*

THE GREAT HALL

Rich people dined in the *great hall*, a large, high-ceilinged room. The lord and older relatives sat at the *high table,* where servants waited on them. Young children and others of a lower rank sat on benches at trestle tables. A servant set each place with spoons, knives, cups, and bread rolls, but no forks. The rich ate from **pewter** or silver plates and drank from **goblets.** They ate most foods with their fingers, so **pages** carried around jugs of water and napkins for washing up. The layouts of later medieval halls are known from surviving buildings, such as the medieval Guildhall in London. This building has a grand entrance hall that was built in

This fourteenth century great hall at Penshurst Palace, Kent, is 62 feet (19 meters) long and 60 feet (18 m) high.

1411 and below-ground **undercrofts** where goods and foods would have been stored and prepared.

Glossary

archaeologists people who dig up and study ancient objects to learn about the past

excavation hole formed by digging

goblets drinking vessels on stems and without handles

pages medieval waiters or attendants

pewter silver-gray metal made of tin and lead

spits metal sticks for holding meat over a fire as it cooks

undercrofts the lowest floors of medieval stone buildings, used for storage

venison deer meat

CASE STUDY

Everyone enjoyed feasting on holy days.

Feasts

The Christian church set aside certain *holy days* for feasts or festivals. On these days, everyone had the day off of work and took part in the celebrations. Feasts were held outside or in the great houses and were prepared by many servants. Meals could include ten or more courses — and some had up to one hundred! People drank beer, cider, and wine. This source shows that feasts took lots of planning and expense:

And first: one hundred well-fattened cattle, one hundred and thirty sheep, also well fattened, one hundred and twenty pigs; and for each day during the feast, one hundred little piglets, both for roasting and for other needs, and sixty salted large well fattened pigs for larding and making soups.*

*Source: Terence Scully, "Du Fait de Cuisine par Maistre Chiquart," France, 1420

See also: Town Life 8–9, Country Life 10–11, Health and Medicine 16–17, Trade, Craft, and Communications 28–29

Health and Medicine

Men and women living in medieval times faced far more pain and suffering than most people do today. The church taught them that by repenting to God, any illness would be cured. Other medical ideas were based on **astrology**. Doctors, **apothecaries**, nuns, and **midwives** did their best to treat patients with herbs, simple **surgeries**, and nursing care.

MEDICINE

Medieval doctors used many different treatments. Some tried spells and charms or ointments made from dung, blood, and animal fat.

Doctors believed that some diseases were caused because the patient had too much blood. So they made cuts in the patient's veins to let the *extra* blood drain away, or they put **leeches** on the body to suck out the blood. To cure headaches, surgeons sometimes cut a hole in the skull — a process called *trephination*. One medieval medical school, the School of Salerno, had this advice on public health:

Drinke not much wine,
sup light, and soone arise,
From care his head to
keepe, from wrath his
*heart.**

Medieval medical treatments were very dangerous. Medical instruments were unsterilized and generally crude.

*Source: "Salerno Book of Health," Italy, c. eleventh century

Word Discovery

ailment *bodily illness*
anaesthetic *drug given to numb pain before a medical procedure*

anatomy *science dealing with the structure of the body*
antiseptic *mixture that kills germs*

infected *made sick by disease-producing virus or germ*
science *knowledge through study and experiments*

ALCHEMY

Alchemy was the first kind of chemistry. Alchemists believed that if certain substances were mixed together at certain temperatures, the resulting mixture could cure people. Many alchemists also believed that magic played a part in healing the sick. Cures could be bought from alchemists, who first asked questions about a person's **symptoms** before making up the cure. The following describes the process of preparing the *philosopher's stone*, which was believed to cure anyone who was sick:

This illustration from a fourteenth-century manuscript shows an alchemist teaching a pupil the secrets of alchemy.

*Our dissolving water therefore carries with it a great **tincture**, and a great melting or dissolving; because that when it feels the vulgar fire, if there be in it the pure and fine bodies of sol or luna, it immediately melts them, and converts them into its white substance such as itself is, and gives to the body color, weight, and tincture.**

*Source: "Secret Book of Artephius," France, twelfth century

Glossary

alchemy medieval chemistry; preparation of chemicals to produce medicines
apothecaries people who prepare and sell medicines
astrolabe a device used to see and figure the position of stars and planets at different times
astrology study of how planets and stars influence human lives
leeches flat worms that suck blood
melancholy sadness or depression
midwives people who assist with childbirth
surgeries procedures that involve cutting the body to cure injuries or illnesses
symptoms signs of illness
tincture a type of medicine

See also: Religion 6–7, Death 12–13, Food and Drink 14–15, Men and Women 18–19

CASE STUDY

Astrology

People believed in astrology — that the stars and planets had a direct influence on their lives. Cures or formulas were believed to have a better effect if taken or mixed up at particular times. For example, one medieval medical book records that:

*Saturn seems to have impressed the seal of **melancholy** on me from the beginning; set, as he is, almost in the midst of my ascendant Aquarius, he is influenced by Mars, also in Aquarius, and the Moon in Capricorn. He is in square aspect to the Sun and Mercury in Scorpio, which occupy the ninth house.**

Medieval astrologers used a device called an **astrolabe** to know when sunrise or sunset would fall and to figure out the position of the Sun and stars in the sky.

Astrolabes, such as this English one from 1326, were used for studying stars and planets.

*Source: Letter of Ficino to Giovanni Cavalacanti, quoted in Marsilio Ficino, "Three Books on Life," Italy, 1489

Men and Women

Few people in medieval Europe could read and write. Because most of those who could do so were men, most medieval information comes from the male viewpoint. Some women were well known. When women married, however, they usually spent most of their lives having and looking after children. Marriages tended to last for life, but that did not mean what it does today. Disease and the hazards of childbirth meant that a marriage of ten to fifteen years was a long one.

MARRIAGE AND CHILDREN

Among rich people, marriages were like business deals because the wealth, position, and political power of their spouse and his or her family mattered most.

Most wealthy people married someone who was chosen by their parents.

There were strict social codes that people were expected to follow. For example, it was outlined in the *Magna Carta* that:

*Heirs may be given in marriage, but not to someone of lower social standing. Before a marriage takes place, it shall be made known to the heir's **next-of-kin**.**

Young people usually married when they were between twelve and fifteen years old. It also became **fashionable** for a knight to choose a married woman and love her from a distance. The knight would fight for her in battles and **tournaments**. This behavior became known as *courtly love*. Having children was important to married people. One reason for this in poorer families was that children could help with the household chores and farm work and look after younger siblings. Children in peasant families were more likely to help their parents at home than to go to school. Most schools had no books. Sometimes, classes had as many as one hundred students, and the school day could be up to thirteen hours long.

*Source: Magna Carta, England, 1215

Word Discovery

captive *taken and kept as a prisoner*

culture *arts and customs of*

a society or country

founded *set up or started building*

scholars *learned and educated people; students*

troops *soldiers or armed forces*

FAMOUS PEOPLE

The tale of **legendary** English folk hero Robin Hood, who robbed from the rich to give to the poor, is said to have been based on real people. This extract is in the original middle-English language:

*But Robyn toke out a too-hond sworde, That hangit down be his kne; Ther as the schereff and his men stode thyckust, Thedurwarde wolde he.**

Both Christopher Columbus and Marco Polo led explorations to other continents, including parts of Asia and the Americas. Famous medieval writers include Christine de Pisan, a French woman who wrote many books, including history and poetry. Geoffrey Chaucer was probably the most famous writer from the Middle Ages. His best-known book was *The Canterbury Tales*, which he began writing in about 1387. It was one of the first books to be printed in England — over one hundred years later.

The first written account of Robin Hood can be dated back to 1420.

*Source: "Robin Hood and the Monk," England, c. 1450. Translated into modern English, this passage would read something like this: "Robin took out his two-handed sword, That hung down to his knees; And as the sheriff and his men stood strong, Robin rushed forward."

Glossary

burned at the stake tied to a pole over a bonfire, which was then lit

fashionable in style, popular

heirs people entitled to the property of another after their death

heresy a belief that goes against the teachings or principles of a religion

legendary related to a legend, which is a story from the past that is believed to be true but cannot be proved

next-of-kin person's closest living relative

tournaments medieval fights between knights on horseback using blunted weapons in front of large crowds

CASE STUDY

Joan of Arc was burned at the stake for her beliefs. This image comes from an illumination in a French book from the fifteenth century.

Joan of Arc

Joan of Arc was a French peasant girl who said she heard the voices of Christian saints. She led the French army to victory over the English. Soon after, however, the Burgundians captured and sold her to the English. She was accused of **heresy**, put on trial as a witch, and **burned at the stake**. Today, Joan is recognized by the Roman Catholic Church as a saint. Most of what is known about Joan of Arc comes from the official records of her 1431 trial. Throughout the trial, she insisted that she heard the voices of saints:

*... if I saw the fire lighted, the faggots prepared, and the executioner ready to kindle the fire, and if I myself were in the fire, I would not say otherwise, and would maintain to the death all I have said.**

*Source: Transcripts of Joan of Arc's Trial, England, 1431

See also: Religion 6–7, Health and Medicine 16–17, Crime and Punishment 20–21, Penance and Pilgrimages 30–31

Crime and Punishment

There was a court system in the Middle Ages through which most convicted criminals were punished with **fines**. However, punishments could also be violent and cruel. There were very few prisons, and a serious **crime** would often result in the death penalty. When the courts could not decide if someone was guilty or not, it was left for God to decide in the form of a judicial ordeal.

COURTS AND TRIALS

The body of a peasant who had been hung might be left on a gibbet as a warning to others. This illustration comes from a 1480 German manuscript.

Small crimes were tried in local courts. Poor people who were caught begging were **flogged** or put in the **stocks**. Thieves had their hands cut off, and violent crimes were punished by beheading, burning at the stake, or hanging.

Most medieval towns had a **gibbet** outside where people were hanged and the bodies of people **executed** were left to rot as a warning to others. The locations of these **gallows** are known from place-names that still exist today, such as Dead Man's Oak or Gallows Hill. *Judicial ordeal* meant that the person on trial was made to suffer a terrifying experience that usually involved fire or boiling water. People believed that if the person was innocent, God would perform a miracle to save him. Judicial ordeal was banned by the church in 1215. In 1232, the **Inquisition** was begun to hunt for people who disagreed with the teachings of the Catholic Church. Anyone found guilty by the Inquisition might be **tortured**. A source from the period describes an Inquisition torture session:

... the inquisitor ordered that, dressed in a short tunic, the prisoner be put first in a bath of hot water, then of cold. Then, with a stone tied to his feet, he was raised up again, kept there for a while, and dropped again, and his shins were poked with reeds as sharp as swords.*

*Source: Angelo Clareno, "An Inquisitional Torture Session," Italy, 1304

THE PEASANTS' REVOLT

In the summer of 1381, **revolts** broke out in parts of England after the introduction of a **poll tax**. The rebels went to London, where they killed church ministers. Then, the Mayor of London killed the peasant leader of the revolt, who was named Wat Tyler. An account from the time describes the event of Tyler's death:

And the Mayor went thither and found him, and had him carried out to the middle of Smithfield, in presence of his fellows, and there beheaded. And thus ended his wretched life. But the Mayor had his head set on a pole and borne before him to the King ...*

Hundreds of peasants died during the revolt, but it caused later governments to give peasants a fairer arrangement.

This illustration shows the execution of Archbishop Simon of Sudbury and Sir Robert Hales at Tower Hill during the Peasants' Revolt of 1381.

*Source: Anonimalle Chronicle, "English Peasants' Revolt," England, 1381

CASE STUDY

The Battle of Bosworth Field was recorded by many medieval writers and artists.

Killing of a King

In August 1485, two English armies confronted each other at Bosworth Field in England. One was led by King Richard III and the other by Henry Tudor, Earl of Richmond. Two hours later the king's army was defeated, Richard was dead, and his crown lay in a thorn bush. Lord Stanley picked up the crown and placed it on Henry Tudor's head. He was now Henry VII, King of England. A ballad by an eye-witness describes the moment:

... the crowne of gold that was bright, to the Lord Stanley deliuered itt bee. Anon to King Henry deliuered it hee ... & said, "methinke ye are best worthye to weare the crowne and be our King."*

*Source: Anonymous, "Ballad of Bosworth Field", England, late sixteenth century

Glossary

crime act that is against the law
executed killed as punishment
fines money paid as a punishment
flogged beaten with a whip or a stick
gallows another name for a gibbet
gibbet wooden structure to hang people on; also known as a gallows
Inquisition church hunt for heretics

poll tax a tax on the people
revolts trying to overthrow the king or people in power by force; to turn against
stocks wooden frame with holes for locking arms, neck, and sometimes feet, used as a punishment in the center of a town
tortured being severely hurt as punishment or as pressure to reveal information

See also: Rulers and Power 4–5, Town Life 8–9, Death 12–13, Men and Women 18–19

The Crusades

The Crusades were a series of wars that Christians started so they could try to regain control of the city of Jerusalem and the holy land of Palestine, which had become part of the Muslim **empire**. Eight main Crusades took place from 1096 to 1291, when the **Muslims** finally drove the Christians out. Although the Crusades were not a success for the Christians, their contact with **Arab** civilizations taught Europeans many new things about building and warfare. They also discovered carpets and sugar and learned about stars, mathematics, and medicine.

CRUSADERS AND SARACENS

This nineteenth century illustration shows Richard I leaving with his soldiers to join the Crusades.

Crusaders came from all over Europe. Some joined bands of fighting monks, such as the Knights of St. John or the Knights Templar.

Muslim soldiers of the holy land were called Saracens and included Arabs, Turks, and Kurds. Their most famous leader was named Saladin, and he earned the respect of many Crusaders. His capture of Jerusalem in 1187 started the bloody Third Crusade, led by English king Richard I. A source from the period gives a description of the Third Crusade:

Arrows fell like raindrops, so that one could not show a finger above the ramparts without being hit. There were so many wounded that all the hospitals and physicians in the city were hard put to it just to extract the missiles from their bodies. *

Finally, in 1229, Emperor Frederick II of Germany reclaimed Jerusalem. Rather than fight the Saracens, he made peace with them and persuaded the **sultan** to surrender the holy city. Jerusalem remained in European hands for only fifteen years and was lost completely in 1244. After another forty-seven years of fighting, the Crusades finally ended as a costly failure for the Europeans.

*Source: Anonymous, "The Capture of Jerusalem by Saladin," England, 1187

Word Discovery

coexist *live together in peace*
recapture *capture again*
tolerance *respect for and* *allowance of beliefs or practices that differ or conflict with one's own*

treaty *written agreement between two or more countries or rulers to end a conflict*

JEWS, CHRISTIANS, AND MUSLIMS

*Jews were **persecuted** throughout the Middle Ages because they were not Christian.*

Although most of Europe was Christian, Muslim lands stretched from parts of Spain through North Africa to Central Asia. There were communities of Jews in many parts of Europe, too, because the Romans had **expelled** the **ancestors** of Jews from Jerusalem in A.D. 70. In most of **Christendom**, religious hatred against Muslims and Jews ran high.

Jews had been treated terribly in England, and in 1290, Edward I expelled them. A medieval writer named Albert of Aix wrote about the Christian attacks on Jews:

*… they rose in a spirit of cruelty against the Jewish people scattered throughout these cities and slaughtered them without mercy.**

Source: Albert of Aix, "Emico and the Slaughter of the Rhineland Jews," France, 1096

Glossary

ancestors people from whom one is descended
Arab a native of Arabia; Arabic-speaking person
Christendom places where Christians are in the majority
crusaders Christian soldiers who fought in the Crusades

depopulated no longer many people there
empire lands governed by a single ruler
expelled forced out
Muslims followers of the Islamic religion
persecuted harassed, chased, or punished because of beliefs
sultan Muslim ruler or king
truce agreement to stop fighting

See also: Rulers and Power 4–5, Religion 6–7, Death 12–13, Buildings 26–27

CASE STUDY

Richard the Lionheart

In 1189, Richard I became King of England and the next year he joined the Third Crusade. During the war, Richard became very ill and decided to accept Saladin's peace terms. A source describes the situation:

*As his illness became very grave, the King … chose, as the least inconvenient course, to seek to make a **truce** rather than to desert the **depopulated** land altogether and to leave the business unfinished as all the others had done who left the groups in the ships.**

Even though the Crusade was unsuccessful, Richard was loved by his people. His heroic actions brought him the nickname Coeur de Lion (Lionheart).

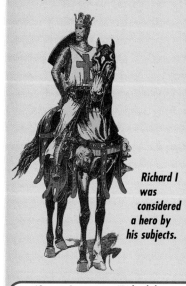

Richard I was considered a hero by his subjects.

Source: Anonymous, "Richard the Lionheart Makes Peace with Saladin," England, 1192

Art

Medieval art is usually divided into two overlapping periods: Romanesque (1050–1180) and Gothic (1150–1550). These names describe the different creative styles and **techniques** used by artists during these times. Most medieval artists were either monks or craftspeople. They rarely signed their works because they made things to honor God or royalty. Artists believed that the person who made the works of art was not important.

ART FOR THE CHURCH

This painting, called the **Wilton Diptych,** *was painted in about 1395. It depicts Richard II worshiping the Virgin Mary and infant Jesus.*

Painters recreated scenes from the Bible on the walls of churches, while **sculptors** carved such scenes on columns, walls, and doors or made statues of holy figures. Metal workers made **chalices**, plates, and crosses, and glass workers produced colorful stained glass windows for the church. Art often pictured frightening scenes that encouraged people to be good Christians rather than risk going to hell. The expensive materials used in art made people realize the importance and power of God. Surviving records of the art owned by churches include the Chantry Certificates of 1547. These certificates list all the objects belonging to private chapels.

Most art, particularly metalwork and sculpture, was created for the church. Church leaders, kings, and noblemen hired artists to produce pictures, statues, and other works to teach people about Christianity.

Word Discovery

adornment adding decoration
icons pictures of the Holy Family or saints
parchment sheep or goat skin

prepared for writing on
plaster a mixture used to make walls smooth
Renaissance period between

the medieval and modern ages, from about 1400–1600, when influence of Greek and Roman ideas was felt in arts and science

MATERIALS AND METHODS

To make paint, artists had to grind **pigments** and then mix them with **resin**, water, egg yolk, or oil. Many recipes for making paint survive, such as this one for making the color red:

*Mingle salt and honny together in a bason, let it stand eight daies, then **seeth** it, and it will be a red color.**

Brushes were made from animal hair or fur that was tied to the quill of a feather or a wooden stick. Sculptors and woodworkers used stone, wood, or marble to make statues. Other craftspeople created with glass, ivory, **enamel**, gold, silver, and bronze, or made **tapestries**, embroideries, or stained glass windows. Clay was used for making pottery or tiles.

Paint was made during the Middle Ages by grinding pigments, such as these.

*Source: "A Booke of Secrets, England," 1596 (translated from Dutch edition of 1531)

Glossary

chalice a wine cup used in a Catholic Mass
embroidery art that adds decorative designs onto cloth using needlework
enamel colored liquid that becomes smooth, shiny, and hard after heating
frescoes paintings done on walls while the plaster is still wet
illuminations manuscript illustrations or letters drawn in elaborate designs that may use gold, silver, or bright colors
pigments colored materials taken from animals, plants, earth, or rocks and used to make paint or dye
resin a liquid made from tree sap
sculptors artists who make art objects by carving, modeling, or welding a hard material, such as stone, wood, or metal
seeth boil gently or soak in a liquid
tapestries thick woven fabrics with pictures of detailed scenes used as wall hangings or curtains or on furniture (The Bayeux Tapestry is actually an **embroidery**.)
techniques methods

CASE STUDY

This detail from the Bayeux Tapestry depicts William of Normandy's ships sailing toward Hastings.

Storytelling Art

Most people in medieval times could not read. Pictures were an important way of telling stories. Much of the art in the Middle Ages told stories from the Bible. One kind of painting that was especially important was the **illuminations** created to illustrate books. Paintings on church walls, called **frescoes**, were also popular. The Bayeux Tapestry is one of the most famous pieces of medieval art because it told the story of William the Conqueror, Harold II, and the Battle of Hastings in 1066. Today, the Bayeux Tapestry is located in Normandy, France.

*Source: You can see details from the Bayeux Tapestry on the Internet at: www.hastings1066.com/baythumb.shtml

See also: Religion 6–7, Buildings 26–27, Trade, Craft, and Communications 28–29, Penance and Pilgrimages 30–31

Buildings

Some of the techniques used for building during the medieval era are still used by **architects** and builders today. **Masons** and architects designed fine buildings that included churches, castles, great houses, and monasteries. The medieval Saint Paul's Cathedral, with its towering wooden **steeple**, was the main landmark of the city of London and the tallest building in Europe. Medieval towns needed strong walls and well-guarded gates to keep attackers out. Most houses, however, did not stay standing longer than fifty years.

HOUSES

Most houses were made of wooden frames with walls made of wattle and daub. After about 1400, many rich people lived in large brick houses with interior walls paneled in wood.

By the end of the medieval period, these houses had large chimneys and occasionally glass windows.

Peasants lived in simple timber-framed houses with wattle and daub walls and only one or two rooms. The floors were only bare earth, windows had shutters but no glass, and there were no chimneys. Fires were lit on stone or tile hearths in the center of the room, with a hole in the roof above used for smoke. Town houses were made of timber, wattle and daub, and sometimes with windows filled with horn. Many town houses had upstairs rooms that overhung the streets. The floors of great buildings were tiled or strewn with **rushes**, or straw, and rugs and carpets were designed as coverings for tables or chests. Masons, woodcarvers, and stonecarvers decorated these more impressive buildings inside and out with carvings and statues on the walls and interior ceilings.

Carpenters are shown making a wooden frame for a house in this illustration from a sixteenth-century manuscript on agriculture.

Word Discovery

bailey *outer wall of a castle*
domes *roofs or ceilings in a hemispherical shape*

elaborate *detailed*
ochre *a brownish yellow color that comes from the earth*

structure *building*
tenants *people who rent buildings or land from a landlord*

CASTLES

Bodiam Castle was built in 1385 and is surrounded by a moat.

When William I took control of Britain, his Norman barons built strong castles as **fortresses**. The earliest castles were built of wood, often on a great mound of earth called a *motte*, with a deep ditch all round. By the twelfth century, many castles had massive stone towers, or **keeps**, surrounded by high walls up to 33 feet (10 m) thick. Windows were narrow slits that were too small for attackers to squeeze through. *Portcullises,* strong, spiked gates that dropped closed from above, protected the entrances. The outsides of castles were probably whitewashed and often brightly painted with colored roof tiles and were not just stone-colored as they exist today.

Glossary

arches curved structures that serve as openings or supports to the building
architects people who design buildings
buttresses thick stone or brick piers built against the outside of a wall to strengthen it
fortress stronghold
keeps towers
masons people who cut, shaped, and built in stone and brick

moat deep ditch around a castle, great house, or town
motte mound
rushes straw scattered on the floors. Sometimes herbs and sweet-smelling flowers were added.
steeple tall tower, often with a spire on top

CASE STUDY

Churches

Many churches and cathedrals built in Europe during the medieval era were constructed in the Romanesque style, which was used from about 1050 to 1180. This style used rounded **arches** above doors and windows. Romanesque churches were built in the shape of a cross. Churches built from about 1180 until the sixteenth century were in the Gothic style. **Buttresses** replaced the heavy pillars of Romanesque churches, with pointed arches, rather than round ones. Interior walls were painted in rich colors, such as blues and reds, and patterned with designs such as stars or swirls. All these features, along with huge stained glass windows, made churches seem filled with light and air. Statues and paintings also decorated the inside.

This stained glass window from Chartres Cathedral in France was made in the thirteenth century.

See also: Rulers and Power 4–5, Religion 6–7, Town Life 8–9, Country Life 10–11

Trade, Craft, and Communications

Much is known about the trades and crafts of the early medieval period because, in 1086, William I sent officials throughout England to find out what jobs people did. The **information** from this **survey** was written down in a great book called the *Domesday Book*. Trading with foreign countries was very important during the Middle Ages, but travel was difficult and dangerous. Merchants traveled across the sea, where they had to be careful of pirates. Even merchants' ships could be dangerous, because they were not safe in rough water.

TRADES AND CRAFTS

The people who practiced a craft usually sold their goods, too. Many people, however, made a living simply through trading alone. These tradesmen and merchants, like craftspeople, lived and worked near markets. Most trades across Europe were controlled by powerful groups of merchants. The largest of these was the Hanseatic League, which was formed in the twelfth century mainly by German merchants. King Henry III gave them permission to set up a base in London. Their ships brought in salted fish, timber, **dyestuffs**, and iron goods. In return, these merchants bought English goods and sold them abroad. Most crafts- and tradespeople belonged to **guilds**. Guilds fined anyone making or selling shoddy goods or anyone whose prices were too high. Here is an example of a rule from the weavers' guild:

*But if any one be caught with false cloth, his cloth will be burned publicly, and verily, the author of the crime will amend according to justice.**

Spinning and weaving were crafts that were generally done by women.

*Source: The Regulations of the Weavers' Gild of Stendal, Germany, 1233

Word Discovery

cogs *merchants' sailing ships*
export *sell in another country*
guildhalls *meeting places for* | *members of crafts guilds*
import *buy from another country* | **warehouses** *buildings for storing goods*

SHIPS AND SAILING

Many medieval towns built waterfronts where ships could dock to unload cargo.

Sailing ships carried goods to and from other countries. Many towns built big timber waterfronts that jutted out into rivers so that **cargo** ships could dock there. Travel and trading improved relationships between countries, and people soon became familiar with foreign produce that they had never seen before. Written accounts say that it was much cheaper for people to transport goods by water than overland in the Middle Ages. The rights of merchants were protected by many rules, such as this one:

Also we decree that if a laden ship should come up the Rhone and should wish to moor at any wharf on the river bank of Arles, then the men of that ship may remove on their own authority, and moor elsewhere, without contradiction, any empty ship which may be without a cargo ...

*Source: "Port of Arles: The Navigation Code", France, 1150

The first printing press in England was set up by William Caxton in 1476.

Books

Medieval books, or **manuscripts**, were written and copied by hand, usually by monks, which was a slow and expensive process. Then, in 1450, a German man named Johannes Gutenberg produced the first printed Bible. The craft of papermaking had come to Europe from the East, and, along with printing, this made books much cheaper to produce. In 1471, an Englishman named William Caxton learned about the new **movable type** printing that had been invented in Korea. He set up his own printing press in Westminster in 1476 and printed copies of nearly one hundred different books.

Glossary

cargo goods carried on a ship; also on an airplane, train, or truck, today
Domesday Book record of a survey of the lands and people of England in 1086
dyestuffs substances used as dye or that produce dye
guilds associations of craftsmen or merchants that enforced standards of good workmanship and trade
information knowledge; facts
manuscripts books written by hand; today, books not yet printed
movable type individual letters that can be moved about to print a page
survey ask questions to gather facts about a group of people, area, or subject

An original Gutenburg Bible can be seen on the British Library's web site at:
www.bl.uk/treasures/gutenberg/homepage.html

See also: Town Life 8–9, Country Life 10–11, Food and Drink 14–15, Art 24–25

Penance and Pilgrimages

The medieval church taught that people should **confess** their sins to a priest. If they were truly sorry, then God would forgive them. The priest might then give them a **penance** to perform, which could be anything from saying a prayer, to helping others, to going on a pilgrimage. A pilgrimage is a journey to a holy place. People also went on pilgrimages to ask for special **favors** or simply to give thanks to God. **Flagellants** were a group of people who punished themselves so that God would forgive their sins.

PILGRIMS

Pilgrims followed special trails across Europe and the Middle East to visit places where important religious events had taken place.

Sometimes, pilgrims paid money to see **shrines**. People believed that shrines had special powers, especially the power of healing. Shrines often contained the bodies of saints or some of their bones, hair, or clothing. One of the most famous accounts of a medieval pilgrimage was Geoffrey Chaucer's *The Canterbury Tales*. Here is an extract from this poem:

*It happened that, in that season, on a day/ In Southwark, at the Tabard, as I lay/ Ready to go on pilgrimage and start/ To Canterbury, full **devout** at heart,/ There came at nightfall to that hostelry/ Some nine and twenty in a company/ Of sundry persons who had chanced to fall/ In fellowship, and pilgrims were they all/ That toward Canterbury town would ride.**

Pilgrims were people who traveled to holy places to seek God's **forgiveness** for their sins.

*Source: Geoffrey Chaucer, "The Canterbury Tales," England, late-fourteenth century

Word Discovery

hallowed *sacred*
pious *very religious*
remorse *sorrow for past actions*

route *the ways or roads of a journey*
souvenir *memento; object that*

serves as a reminder
temple *a building for worship*
traveler *one who goes on a trip*

FLAGELLANTS

This detail from a fifteenth century Italian painting shows flagellants kneeling in prayer.

closer to God. They walked about in groups, singing **psalms** and lashing themselves with whips. They said this was punishment not only for their own sins but also for the sins of the world. These people became known as flagellants. A source from the period describes flagellants in this way:

*They formed circles and beat upon their backs with weighted **scourges**, rejoicing as they did so in loud voices and singing hymns suitable to their **rite** and newly composed for it … They flogged their shoulders and arms, scourged with iron points so **zealously** as to draw blood.**

Some people punished themselves as a way of being

*Source: Jean de Venette, "Journal," France, 1349

CASE STUDY

The Canterbury Tales

Written between 1387 and 1400, Geoffrey Chaucer's *The Canterbury Tales* is about a group of pilgrims traveling to Canterbury. It is a very long poem and draws attention to the foolishness of human nature. The characters in the group include a merchant, a knight, a nun, and a plowman. One of the pilgrims, the Wife of Bath, has been on many pilgrimages, as described in this excerpt:

Three times she'd journeyed to Jerusalem; And many a foreign stream she'd had to stem; At Rome she'd been, and she'd been in Boulogne, In Spain at Santiago, and at Cologne.*

Geoffrey Chaucer
Canterbury Tales

Selected, translated, and adapted by
Barbara Cohen

Illustrated by
Trina Schart Hyman

The Canterbury Tales *was reproduced by hand until the first printed version appeared in the 1470s.*

*Source: Geoffrey Chaucer, The Canterbury Tales, England, late-fourteenth century

Glossary

confess admit or tell; acknowledge a sin
devout deeply religious
favors good will; efforts on one's behalf
flagellants people who beat themselves for religious reasons
forgiveness mercy and pardon for errors
penance religious punishment for sins

pilgrims people who travel to holy places
psalms religious songs or poems
rite religious act or ceremony
scourges whips used for punishment
shrines holy places, usually devoted to a saint
zealously eagerly or passionately

See also: Religion 6–7, Men and Women 18–19, Art 24–25, Trade, Craft, and Communications 28–29

Index

animals 8, 9, 10, 15, 24
apprentices 8, 9
art 24, 25, 26, 27
astrology 16, 17

barons 5, 11, 27
Bible, the 24, 25
bishops 6, 7, 13
books 19, 25, 29, 31
buildings 7, 15, 26, 27

castles 27
children 8, 15, 18
Christianity 6, 22, 23, 24
churches 5, 7, 10, 13, 15, 19,
    20, 21, 24, 25, 26, 27, 30
civil wars 4
courts 20
crafts 8, 24, 25, 28
Crusades 22, 23

death 12, 13, 20
diseases 12, 13, 16, 18
doctors 16
Domesday Book 28

famine 4, 5, 12, 13
farming 8, 9, 10, 11
feasts 15
feudal system 5, 10, 11
fires 19, 26
flagellants 30, 31
food 10, 12, 14, 15

God 6, 7, 13, 16, 20, 24,
    30, 31
government 6, 21
guilds 28

heaven and hell 7, 24
holy days 15

houses 11, 12, 13, 15, 26

Inquisition 20

kings 4, 5, 13, 21, 22, 23, 24
knights 13, 18, 22, 31

land 5, 11
life expectancy 12, 13
London 9, 12, 21

Magna Carta 5, 18
manors 10, 11, 14, 21
manuscripts 6, 7, 13, 20, 29
markets 8, 9, 28
marriages 7, 18
Masses 6, 7
meat 9, 10, 14, 15
medicine 12, 13, 16, 17, 22
merchants 8, 9, 28, 29, 31

monks 6, 24, 29
Muslims 22, 23

nuns 6, 16, 31

peasants 5, 8, 10, 11, 12,
    14, 18, 20, 21, 26, 31
pilgrims/pilgrimages 30, 31
plagues 12, 13
poetry 7, 18, 31
poor/poverty 7, 11, 12, 14,
    18, 20
priests 6
prisons 9, 20

queens 4

reading 9, 18, 25
rich 7, 14, 15, 18, 26

schools 6, 18
ships 25, 28, 29
shrines 30, 31
sins 6, 30, 31
soldiers 5, 19, 21, 22
stars 17, 22
streets 8, 9, 12, 13, 26
surgery 16, 17

taxes 9, 10, 21
toilets 12, 13
torturing 20
towns 6, 7, 8, 9, 11, 14, 20,
    26, 29
trading 8, 9, 28
travel 28, 29, 31

wars 4, 12, 22
witches 19
women 4, 16, 18, 19
writing/writers 7, 18, 19, 23

TIME LINE OF MEDIEVAL EUROPE

A.D. 476-1000
Early medieval period following the fall of the Roman Empire.

1066
William of Normandy invades and conquers England. King Harold is killed at the battle of Hastings and William is crowned king.

1086
The Domesday Book is completed. It contains statistics about the people of England – their jobs and land.

1096
First Crusade begins. The Crusaders were Christian armies from all over Europe who fought to regain lands (Palestine and Jerusalem) captured by the Muslims.

1141
Period of Anarchy when William's grandchildren Matilda and Stephen fight over the crown. Stephen eventually wins.

1147
Second Crusade begins. This Crusade is a failure for the Christians.

1154
Henry II becomes king of England— the first in a long line of Anglo-French kings.

1162
Thomas Becket is made Archbishop of Canterbury and is killed for his belief that the church should rule over the King.

1189
Richard the Lionheart becomes King of

England. Third Crusade begins. King Richard makes a deal with Saladin and certain privileges are granted to Christians.

1202
Fourth Crusade begins. The Crusaders never reach the holy land. Instead, Europeans begin trading their goods for exotic goods from Arab countries.

1215
King John of England is forced to add his seal to the Magna Carta, or Great Charter — a set of rules to ensure the king rules his people in a just way.

1291
The end of the Crusades.

1348
The bubonic plague sweeps Europe killing one out of every three people.

1381
The Peasants' Revolt occurs in England.

1387
Geoffrey Chaucer begins writing The Canterbury Tales.

1429
Joan of Arc leads France in victory over England. She is burned at the stake in 1431.

1485
Henry Tudor defeats and kills Richard III and becomes King of England.